LEGENDS AND...
CAMB...

BRADWELL
BOOKS

Published by Bradwell Books

9 Orgreave Close Sheffield S13 9NP

Email: books@bradwellbooks.co.uk

British Library Cataloguing in Publication Data: a catalogue record
for this book is available from the British Library.

1st Edition

ISBN: 9781910551486

Design by: Andrew Caffrey

Typesetting by: JenksDesign

Photograph Credits: iStock and credited individually

Printer: Hobbs - Brunel Road Totton Hampshire SO40 3WX

CONTENTS

Wicken Fen is a remnant of the marshy country that once covered much of Cambridgeshire, contributing to its rich folklore. It was also one of the haunts of Black Shuck. *iStock*

INTRODUCTION

The folklore and folk tales of the British Isles make for an endlessly fascinating study. A glorious confusion of ancient beliefs has evolved over the millennia thanks to the many different races that have settled here. In England they have included Stone Age and Bronze Age tribes, the Iron Age Celts, Romans, Angles, Saxons, Norsemen and Normans.

Into this cultural melting pot have been thrown any number of superstitions and half-remembered tales of cultural heroes, some real, some mythical, and many a mixture of both.

Our ancestors lived very different lives to those we enjoy today. Most were tied to the land and had an intimate relationship with the seasons and the natural world. Few had travelled further than their nearest market town, while many had never even strayed that far from the rustic landscape they knew so well.

Nevertheless, their seemingly limited existence was coloured with an awareness of another world, one where supernatural beings lived alongside them just out of sight; where illness or death could be brought about not by microbes but by witchcraft; and where heroes and villains from a past age lived again in dramatic legends told down the generations.

In this book you will be introduced to just a taster of the legends and folklore which enlivened the days and nights of Cambridgeshire folk a century or more ago. You will learn strange superstitions about Cambridge and its colleges; encounter the 'Book Fish', Black

Shuck, Hob o'-Lantern and Daddy Witch; and meet pious saints and sinister monks, the mysterious Toadmen, wicked witches and the ghostly knight of Wandlebury. You will also learn about the archaic customs formerly carried out to mark the seasons of the year and the crucial stages in life.

The folklore of Cambridgeshire paints the county as a wonderfully magical place. I hope you enjoy this brief tour through its wonders.

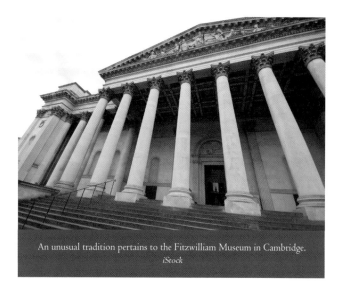

An unusual tradition pertains to the Fitzwilliam Museum in Cambridge.
iStock

TALES OF OLD CAMBRIDGE

Like Rome, Cambridge is traditionally stated as having been founded on seven hills. In such a flat landscape, almost any rise might be considered a hill, but only two really justify the name: Castle Hill and Honey Hill. The other five really are hills in name only. They are Market Hill, St Andrew's Hill, Peas Hill, Pound Hill and Senate House Hill. It must have been even harder to locate seven hills in Norwich, however, another city which claims this distinction. Whoever came up with this conceit in the Middle Ages clearly hoped that some of Rome's ancient glory would rub off on Cambridge (and also on Norwich).

Cambridge became a university town in the 13th century when large numbers of scholars arrived here from Oxford. Their antics had made them so unpopular there that the townsfolk turfed them out. In 1836 Richard Gooch collected together a number of tall tales celebrating the cleverness of Cambridge students, often at the expense of the ordinary townsfolk, who they clearly looked down on. He compiled them into a book called *Facetiae Cantabrigiensis*. A Cambridge student is known as a Cantabrigian (or Cantab, for short).

The stories set down in *Facetiae Cantabrigiensis* had been circulating for many years and formed a body of folklore all their own. However, their content suggests they may well have been invented by the students themselves. The following story, for example, has clearly been borrowed from *The Metamorphoses* of Apuleius, the only Ancient Roman novel to have come down to the modern age. Also known as *The Golden Ass*, it would certainly have been known to any classical scholar.

Writes Richard Gooch: 'A party of Cantabs one day, walking along a street in Cambridge, espied an ass tied to a door, and they resolved to play *bumpkin* a trick, who, having disposed of his wares, was enjoying his pint and his pipe within doors. The Cantabs were not long at a loss what to be at, one of them proposing that the panniers should be put upon his back, and bridle on his head, while the rest led the ass astray. In this condition stood the scholar, when bumpkin, who had by this time finished his pipe and pint, came to the door; all amazement at what he saw, he stood gaping for a minute or two, when the Cantab thus addressed him: "You must know, sir, that I quarrelled with my father about seven years since, and for my disobedience, I was changed into the degrading shape of an ass, to endure every hardship for that space of time; which being now expired, you are bound to set me at liberty."

'Bumpkin, believing the tale, took off the panniers and bridle, and set the scholar at large. A few days after, bumpkin went to a neighbouring country fair to purchase another ass and, to his no small surprise, his old identical ass was offered to him; which, on seeing its master, brayed most piteously in token of recognition; but Hodge, nothing moved thereat, passed on to another, exclaiming – "So you have quarrelled with your father again, have you? But dang me if I'll have you again!"

No wonder the scholars were booted out of Oxford if this is the sort of stunt they got up to!

Cambridge was popularly believed to have been built on seven hills, like Rome.
iStock

There are a number of interesting traditions relating to the colleges. For example, a venerable mulberry tree which grows in the Fellows' Garden of Christ's College is said to have been planted by the poet John Milton to celebrate his graduation in 1633. If so, it is approaching 400 years of age, and yet it still bears fruit. The apparition of a tall man, stooped over as if in despair, his hands clasped behind is back, has allegedly been seen wandering round and round this tree on certain moonlit nights. This is supposed to be the troubled spirit of a Victorian academic, Christopher Round.

According to *A College Mystery*, a book published by A.P. Barker in 1918, Round confessed on his deathbed to a murder no one knew had been committed. He said that one night he happened to come across a man named Philip Collier staggering around the grounds as if he was drunk. Round hated Collier: not only were they bitter academic rivals, they were also rivals in love, for the

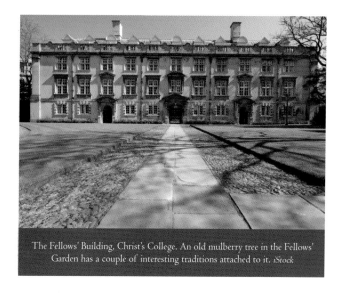

The Fellows' Building, Christ's College. An old mulberry tree in the Fellows' Garden has a couple of interesting traditions attached to it. *iStock*

affections of a girl called Mary Clifford. As Round watched, Collier stumbled and fell into a private swimming pool in the Fellows' Garden. Although he was disgusted by the sight of Collier's supposed drunkenness, he hurried over to help him. He picked up a boathook, intending to use it to drag him out of the water, but then he realised this was an opportunity to get Collier out of the way for good. Almost without thinking, he brought the boathook crashing down on his hated rival's head. He walked away, leaving Collier to drown.

There was a tragic and unlooked-for sequel to this act, however. Unbeknownst to the murderer, Collier had not been drunk that fateful night. He had been experimenting with anaesthetics, a study still then in its infancy. Mary, the girl they both loved, suffered from a progressive illness and Collier had been seeking ways to ease her pain. With his death, of course, the experiments ceased and in time Mary, too, died – in dreadful and perhaps preventable agony. For forty years the remorseful Round took to pacing round Milton's mulberry tree at night, unable to sleep, and his ghost paces there still. That at least is the story, but whether there's any truth in it is open to conjecture.

The architectural gem that is the Wren Library is one of the ornaments of Trinity College. It stands at one end of Nevile's Court. At the other, a great iron knocker can be seen hanging on a door in the cloisters. For many years, it was claimed that if you were to stamp hard on a flagstone near the entrance to Wren's Library, you could make the heavy knocker at the other end strike the door. The sound of its knock would then echo through the courtyard. The particular flagstone has a heel-shaped depression in it, possibly caused by people repeatedly trying to create the phenomenon.

In 1910, the Revd Edward Conybeare noted: 'So great a part does this illusion play in human impressions, that five out of six, when

The Wren Library in Nevile's Court, Trinity College. Can you make the knocker knock? *iStock*

they hear this sound, are ready to declare that they have seen the knocker actually move.' In her 1969 book *Cambridgeshire Customs and Folklore*, author Enid Porter writes that she was convinced she saw the knocker move when she stamped on the flagstone as a child. However, the trick was to stamp facing the library, so that you had to spin round in order to see the knocker fall. If you tried it the other way round, the magic wouldn't work. This game amused Cambridge children for decades.

When it works, the 'knock' is actually an echo created by the peculiar acoustics of Nevile's Court. The Revd Mr Conybeare states: 'It was by timing this echo … that Sir Isaac Newton first measured the velocity of sound.'

The magnificent stone lions guarding the main entrance to the Fitzwilliam Museum feature in an even stranger tradition. It used to be said that when they heard the clock of the nearby Catholic church strike midnight, they would roar! Another variant is that they would step down from their plinths and drink from the water running through the gutters in Trumpington Street. This latter version echoes very old traditions of prehistoric standing stones which were said to magically move from their positions at certain times of the year to drink from sacred springs and wells. The origins of such beliefs are lost in the mists of time but might refer to some ancient pagan ritual.

THE GOGMAGOGS

Just to the south of Cambridge are the oddly named Gogmagog Hills. The derivation is uncertain but may be linked to the name of a mythical giant. Geoffrey of Monmouth, in his 12th-century *History of the Kings of Britain*, recounts a tale of a giant called Goemagot, which in later versions became Gogmagog. In the Guildhall in London there stand the effigies of two giants, known as Gog and Magog. By the 17th century, the students of Cambridge had taken to digging a representation of the giant in the turf at or near Wandlebury Camp. By this time 'Gogmagog' had become a generic term for a giant, and turf-cut hill figures elsewhere in England were given the same name.

In the 1950s, archaeologist T.C. Lethbridge claimed to have discovered traces of a series of hill figures formerly cut into the Gogmagogs. He believed they were more than a thousand years old and suggested they may have been linked to pagan fertility rites. He thought these may have continued after a fashion into the 16th century, when they would simply have taken the form of 'pastimes', in other words a fair and country sports. It is known that in 1574 the students of Cambridge were banned from attending these pastimes because of their debased nature. Although the alleged discovery of these 'buried gods' caused a sensation, the Council for British Archaeology cast doubts on Lethbridge's research and later studies showed that in many areas the soil had never been removed, even centuries ago. No sign of the supposed gods and goddesses have come to light since, but it's possible that the students' 16th- and 17th-century depiction of Gogmagog may still lie under the turf somewhere.

The statue of Gog in the Guildhall in London. His companion Magog stands nearby. The Gogmagog Hills appear to be named after the same mythical giants.

Along the tops of the Gogmagog Hills the ramparts of an ancient hill fort are clearly seen. This is Wandlebury Camp, a large Iron Age fortification, circular in plan. The plan of the hill fort was partly destroyed when local bigwig Lord Godolphin decided to build a mansion within it and carried out extensive landscaping work. Only one stable block survives of this undertaking, however, together with a monument dedicated to Lord Godolphin's favourite racehorse. According to the authors of *The Lore of the Land*, Jacqueline Simpson and Jennifer Westwood, the name 'Wandlebury' dervies from the Anglo-Saxon personal name Wændel, who may possibly be another mythical giant, for the famous chalk carving on the South Coast, the Long Man of Wilmington, was known more than a millennium ago as 'the helmeted Wændel'. Perhaps this is the true name of the 'Gogmagog' cut out of the chalk by Cambridgeshire scholars.

In the 13th century the monkish scholar Gervase of Tilbury set down a romantic legend about Wandlebury Camp which featured an anonymous ghostly knight, who might perhaps be another folk memory of the long-forgotten Wændel. Even 700 or so years ago, Gervase described the legend as 'a very ancient tradition'.

He wrote: 'If a warrior enters this level space [behind the ramparts] at dead of night, when the moon is shining, and cries "Knight to Knight, come forth!" immediately he will be confronted by a warrior, armed for fight, who, charging horse to horse, either dismounts his adversary or is dismounted. But I should add that the warrior must enter the enclosure alone, although his companions may look on from outside.'

One of those who chose to test himself against the Wandlebury knight was a Norman warrior by the name of Osbert Fitzhugh. Fitzhugh had been staying at Cambridge Castle when he learnt of the existence of the ghostly knight. When the moon was full and bright, he trotted off to Wandlebury Camp with his squire in tow. Leaving his squire outside the ramparts, Fitzhugh rode in and called out loudly: 'Knight to Knight come forth!' Out of the darkness emerged a knight – 'or what appeared to be a knight'. The two warriors immediately set to, their blows resounding through the night air. It was a fierce fight and went on for quite some time, but the mortal knight ultimately proved victorious. He succeeded in unhorsing his mystical opponent.

Much struck by the power and beauty of the ghostly knight's mount – a magnificent black stallion – Fitzhugh decided to keep the horse as his fair spoils. Without a backward glance, he began to lead the animal out of the encampment. The phantom knight was not quite done, however. From where he lay on the ground, he hurled his spear, piercing Fitzhugh's thigh. But this was not enough to prevent the Norman from making his way out beyond the ramparts.

Back at Cambridge Castle, Osbert Fitzhugh tethered the Wandlebury knight's horse in the courtyard and then went to have his wound dressed. At cockcrow the following morning, the black stallion suddenly reared up, snorted furiously and with a tremendous effort snapped the reins that held it. Then it galloped away through the castle gates, never to be seen again. Fitzhugh was left with a less welcome reminder of his encounter with the Wandlebury knight, however. Every year on the anniversary of their battle, the wound in his thigh would reopen and bleed.

Two views of the rampart round Wandlebury Camp, where a ghostly knight would challenge all-comers. © Joe McIntyre and Simon Middleton

PECULIAR HISTORIES

A romantic medieval legend, offered as genuine history, claims to provide the origin of the name of the village of Littleport, near Ely. In his book *Tales from the Fens*, author W.H. Barrett sets down the legend as told to him by an old Fenman with the wonderfully archaic name of Chafer Legge. Mr Legge explained that, many centuries ago, King Canute was staying with the monks of Ely and he decided to take a punt and catch some eels because his wife the queen was particularly partial to them. (Canute, or more properly, Cnut, ruled England and also Denmark, Norway and parts of Sweden in the early 11th century). Unfortunately, the wind blew up and the king found himself in difficulties. The punt ran aground.

King Canute struggled out of the mud and through a reed bed until he came to a hut belonging to a poor man who worked on the monks' farm. The man introduced himself as Legres – he was Mr Legge's distant ancestor – and he welcomed in the bedraggled stranger, setting him to warm by the fire and offering him a plate of eel stew. He had no idea he was entertaining royalty. Later Legres took Canute to the abbey farm, but the monk who opened the door to them did anything but welcome them. He had no reason to know he was addressing anyone other than a couple of serfs. He told them to be off, for he and his brothers were too busy enjoying a feast to be bothered with the likes of them. He added that if they didn't make themselves scarce, he would set the dogs on them.

The king was understandably appalled. Following Legres back to his hut, he learnt this was not the first time his humble host had been so treated. Legres told Canute that some years previously the monks had abducted his wife. When he tried to get her back, the monks flogged him and then set the dogs on the pair of them. His wife was killed and he barely got away with his life. Legres admitted that in revenge for his wife's murder he had found a way of secretly disposing of a monk every year on the anniversary of the birthday of their little son. The 'son' was now eighteen years of age, but the next morning Canute happened upon his host's child bathing in a stream and saw that she was in fact his daughter — and a very beautiful one at that. She had taken to wearing boys' clothes to hide herself from the monks' lustful attentions.

By this time King Canute's men had been searching for him. Once they were reunited, the king launched an attack on the abbey farm. He burned it to the ground, while Legres stood at the exit, hacking at every fleeing monk with his sword. Canute then took the Bishop of Ely to task for his laxity. At the bishop's expense, a new house was built for Legres, who was made a freeman and the royal brewer. Those monks who had survived were set to work for Legres in the brewery. The king's nephew married Legres's beautiful daughter.

Rounding up the story, Mr Legge explained that it was still the custom to name the first-born son in his family Canute. The king renamed the settlement where the adventure occurred 'Littleport' because it had proved a little port for him when he was caught in a storm. He also named the hill where he ran aground Punt Hill.

It is difficult to know now how much true history there is in this yarn of Mr Legge's, but early medieval England was a wild, uncertain place and its rulers all fairly maverick, more than willing to wield a sword and take matters into their own hands. So there may be some truth in it.

The best-known story of King Canute is the one in which he demonstrates that even kingly power cannot hold back the tide. The king also got his feet wet at Littleport, but this was just the beginning of an exciting adventure involving corrupt monks and cross-dressing serfs. *iStock*

More historical but somewhat stranger is the story of Elizabeth Woodcock. In the winter of 1799 Mrs Woodcock was returning on horseback from Cambridge when a blizzard blew up. She succeeded in struggling through the snow until almost in sight of her home village of Impington but then something extraordinary happened. A meteor fell out of the sky, startling her horse. Mrs Woodock was thrown out of her saddle and into a snow drift with such force that she was knocked unconscious. When she awoke, she found that she was now trapped inside a hollow space, a kind of snow-cave. The poor woman only had some snuff and a bag of nuts to sustain her. Fortunately, she also had a nutcracker.

Mrs Woodcock survived inside this icy prison for nine days before she was eventually rescued, on 10 February. Tragically, she was so badly frostbitten that she lost all her fingers and toes. The shock proved too much for her and she died several months later. Mrs Woodcock was buried in Impington churchyard, where there is a memorial describing her ordeal. I believe her nutcrackers are still held as a memento in Cambridge and County Folk Museum.

There is another bizarre anecdote about a young man in Cambridge who attempted to enter the local record books by stuffing his face with way too much food. He succeeded in winning the champion glutton title in the year 1770 by forcing down eight pounds of mutton, with all the trimmings. However, this was not enough for the jaded appetites of the people of Cambridge, who had seen this sort of spectacle once too often already. Goaded on by their greed for sensation, the youth next made a demonstration of his eating prowess on 29 August. On this occasion he disgusted everyone by dining off a cat garnished with onions!

Monks had a bad reputation in medieval lore and literature for living ungodly lives devoted to sensual pleasures such as eating and drinking instead of to prayer. The monks of Ely in Mr Legge's story upheld that tradition. *iStock*

HOLY WONDERS

An extraordinary little book was published in 1627, describing a remarkable cod that found its way on to a slab in Cambridge market. *Vox Piscis: Or the Book-Fish* tells how a fishmonger, on cutting up the fish, found in its gullet 'a booke … much soyled, and defaced, and covered over with a kind of slime & congealed matter'. It was wrapped in a sheet of canvas. The remarkable discovery was brought to the attention of several Cambridge worthies and it was taken to the vice-chancellor of the university.

On examination the book was found to be a religious work, containing three essays written by the 16th-century Protestant reformer John Frith while he was languishing in a makeshift prison in Oxford. Frith got into trouble as a student for being in possession of what were then considered heretical books. He later became friends with William Tyndale, the man who translated the Bible into English, and was finally burned at the stake in 1533 for refusing to acknowledge doctrines key to the Roman Catholic faith. It is a further tragedy that if he had avoided punishment for a few more years, his views would have found favour with the reformations carried out by Henry VIII when he broke with the church in Rome.

It was an extra curiosity that when Frith wrote the tracts found within the 'book-fish', he was being held in a cellar that was also used to store fish. Although this coincidence excited further speculation, it was generally agreed that its discovery 'is to bee accounted rather marvellous than miraculous', in other words it had not found its way there through a divine agency. Those who examined the book noted that its pages were exceedingly brittle, which they thought might have been due to its being inside the cod long enough for the heat of its body to dry them out.

The author of *Vox Piscis* concluded: 'Therefore it seemeth most probable, that upon some wrack this booke lying (perhaps manie years) in the pocket of some man, that was cast away, was swallowed by the Cod, and that it lay for a good space of time in the fishes belly.'

Although the story is not impossible, it's more likely to have been a hoax. For one thing, too many scholars claimed to have seen the fish being opened. Another, more honest, pointed out that this operation occurred on the fish stall, and that only afterwards was the book brought to anyone's attention. There is a long tradition of tales of wondrous things found in fishes, some of a religious nature. Possibly *Vox Piscis* was a donnish joke or an attempt by someone to further elevate John Frith's reputation.

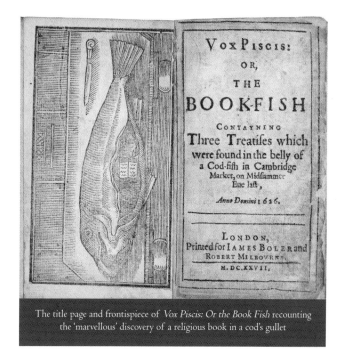

The title page and frontispiece of *Vox Piscis: Or the Book Fish* recounting the 'marvellous' discovery of a religious book in a cod's gullet

We turn now to a more august personage. According to tradition, the East Anglian princess Etheldreda was married twice, but preserved her virginity throughout both relationships. After her second husband, Ecgfrith, King of Northumberland, decided he'd had enough of a wife who insisted on living with him as a sister, this saintly lady retired into a convent at Coldingham in Scotland. However, sometime later Ecgfrith changed his mind – perhaps he needed an heir – and rode up to Coldingham with the intention of forcing Etheldreda to become his wife in more than just name. She made her escape, hotly pursued by her enraged husband. She took refuge at a place on the Berwickshire coast called St Abb's Head, which unexpectedly – some suggested miraculously – became cut off from the mainland by unusually high seas. Ecgfrith was unable to reach her for a whole week and finally took the hint and gave up. The seas soon afterwards subsided and Etheldreda returned to Cambridgeshire.

Etheldreda withdrew to the Isle of Ely, which she had inherited from her first husband. Here she founded a so-called 'double monastery', housing both monks and nuns in different buildings, and served as its abbess. The fame of this religious house went far and wide and eventually led to the construction of Ely Cathedral on the same site. In part this was due to the discovery that, sixteen years after her death in 679, Etheldreda's body was found not to have decayed, a sure sign of saintliness. Her sister, who had taken over as abbess, decided Etheldreda deserved a finer coffin than the one she had been interred in. A splendid Roman sarcophagus had recently been found near Grantchester and the abbess ordered it to be brought to Ely to take Etheldreda's remarkably well-preserved corpse. Her body was found to fit the ancient marble sarcophagus perfectly, which was considered another sign of favour from above.

In time Etheldreda was canonised and Ely became a popular destination for medieval pilgrims. The saint had died of a tumour in her throat, which she had considered a just punishment for her vanity in the days before she joined a nunnery, for she had had a particular love of jewelled necklaces. Those who were suffering from complaints of the throat felt drawn to pray at St Etheldreda's shrine for this reason.

In later centuries St Etheldreda's name became corrupted to the easier to pronounce 'Audrey'. St Audrey's Fair was held in Ely every year on 17 October and here cheap and gaudy lace collars were sold in a vague tribute to Etheldreda's love of necklaces. These were known as St Audrey's Lace, which in turn became shortened to

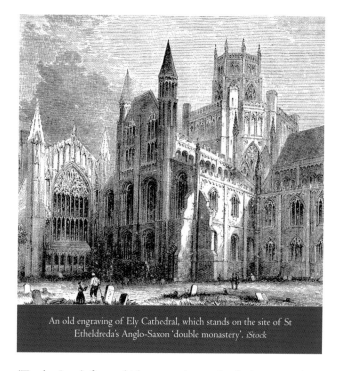

An old engraving of Ely Cathedral, which stands on the site of St Etheldreda's Anglo-Saxon 'double monastery'. *iStock*

'Tawdry Lace', from which we get the word referring to anything showy but worthless.

Sunken Church Field was the odd name given to a parcel of land at a farm in the village of Abington. The name was entirely descriptive, however, for local legend had it that a church formerly stood in the field, but it became abandoned and over many years fell into ruins and became buried. Adding spice to what may have been a memory of a genuine incident were rumours that the ringing of the old church bells and the singing of a ghostly choir could be heard below the ground in Sunken Church Field. It was a place that tended to be avoided after dark.

Similar folk tales occur in other parts of the UK. There is a stone circle in Cumbria called Sunkenkirk, for example. Such names might perhaps refer to sacred sites that predated Christianity, with legends being made up to explain why they were so called.

A grim tradition which might also recall a genuine historical event is attached to the churchyard at Chrishall. There is evidence that an earlier community was originally located further up the hill from where the current village stands. Bits of brick and tile found in the soil bear testimony to the existence of this 'Old Chrishall', which was said to have been destroyed by fire centuries ago in order to purge it of a plague. The tradition further states that the bodies of the plague victims were buried together in a pit in the churchyard. For many years there was a ban on burying bodies where the plague pit had supposedly been dug, for fear of 'letting out the plague'.

Much more cheerful is the tale of a Gypsy named Charlie Gray at Holy Trinity Church in Balsham. Gray asked to be buried alongside the church door, 'because he thought it would be lively on Sundays when the folks gossiped there'.

The 12th-century historian Henry of Huntingdon tells an exciting story about this church, parts of which are Saxon in origin. In his *Historia Anglorum*, Henry recounts the tale of 'The Brave Man of Balsham' who set up a single-handed resistance against invading Vikings. According to Henry, in the year 1010 the Danes spent three months raiding East Anglia and the Fenland, plundering villages, destroying churches and setting fires to crops. Urged on by their leader Sweyn Forkbeard, they torched Cambridge and then headed back over the Gogmagog Hills until they came upon Balsham. Here they put all the adults to the sword and enjoyed themselves by tossing children in the air and catching them on the points of their spears. But one man – 'worthy of far-flung fame' –

Viking marauders murdered everyone at Balsham, except one man whose heroic actions earned him the name of 'The Brave Man of Balsham'. *iStock*

escaped the assault and managed to mount the church tower. From here he single-handedly defended himself from the entire Danish horde until help came.

St George's Church, Thriplow, stands on the hill overlooking the village, and is a bit of a climb to get to. The villagers originally intended to build it in a more convenient spot but halfway through the building work they were amazed to find that the masonry had inexplicably found its way up to the top of the hill. The job of carting all those heavy stones back down the hill was just too daunting, so the villagers took the supernatural hint and continued building the church where it stands today.

In Cottenham a similar story was told of All Saints' Church. Cottenham is a linear village and the church stands at its northernmost end, inconvenient for those who live at the southern end. In this version of the tale, the villagers tried to dismantle the church and move it to a more central position, but every night the masonry was found to have returned to its original location.

Such traditions are centuries old and may recall the earliest period of Christianity in England when the new religion was taking over sites sacred to the old beliefs. Many hilltops were considered sacred places by our pagan ancestors. Perhaps for this reason the mysterious supernatural agency interfering with church building was firmly identified as the Devil. When, for example, the people of March decided to build a church near the Market Place, the Devil, naturally inimical to church building, tore down overnight all the building work that had been done during the day. Eventually the townsfolk erected a cross on the building site and this was enough to ward off the Devil. The church was duly built.

The base of an ancient preaching cross can be found beside the road leading from the Market Place to the church of St Wendreda, and the story may have been told to explain its presence. However, the story appears to be referring to the church built in the newer part of the town in the mid-19th century. If so, this would make the March legend a remarkably recent one for a tale of this type.

Finally, there is a unique tradition belonging to the village of Shingay which might belong in this chapter as much as anywhere. The legend refers to a 'fairy cart' that would magically transport the bodies of the recently dead to Shingay. This was a folk memory of a genuine period in Cambridgeshire's history when Bad King John placed a temporary ban on the religious rites associated with the burial of the dead. Certain religious orders were exempt from this 'Inderdict', as it was known, including the Knights Hospitallers. The Hospitallers had a preceptor at Shingay, and here Mass could continue to be observed and bodies interred in consecrated ground.

A number of churches, or the stones being used to construct them, were moved about by a mysterious agency, which some assumed to be the Devil

While the Inderdict lasted, people from miles around brought their deceased loved ones to Shingay, so that they could be decently buried at the preceptory. The cart which was used to transport the bodies was called a *feretorium*, the pronunciation of which may have suggested 'fairy' to country people of later generations.

THE FEAR OF WITCHCRAFT

For many centuries it was believed that misfortune, illness and even death could be willed upon a person by another skilled in mystic arts or who had been given the power to do so by the Devil. Because witchcraft appears in the Bible (for example, in the story of the Witch of Endor and the conjuring up of a demon for King Solomon), the 'dark arts' were believed in as firmly by educated people as by the illiterate.

It might seem the height of foolish ignorance to believe in witchcraft but it should be remembered that, prior to the 18th century, almost nothing was understood about the causes of disease. Microbes were unknown. We believe in the virus giving us a cold even though we have never seen it and our ancestors believed in the existence of witchcraft with the same degree of certainty.

So firm was the belief in witchcraft that someone accused of cursing an animal or human to fall ill or die was treated just the same as if they had poisoned or murdered their victim by more orthodox means. The criminal justice system saw no difference: the end result was all that mattered. By the dawn of the 17th century, however, Europe had fallen into the grip of a 'witch mania', fuelled in part by the resurgence of bubonic plague and by religious insecurity fanned by the Renaissance. No one was safe from being accused of being a witch. Lonely old women, especially those who had previously been known to provide herbal remedies, harmless love charms and the like, were early targets but even the nobility found themselves accused, often by the unscrupulous as a means of getting them out of the way. Thousands of supposed witches and male sorcerers were hanged or burned alive as the mania swept through Europe.

Cambridgeshire appears to have escaped the worst of the panic, with very few trials for witchcraft being recorded. However, in Huntington, which is now in Cambridgeshire, an early trial for witchcraft took place. In 1593 Alice Samuel, her daughter Agnes and her husband John were hanged for bewitching the wife of local bigwig Lord Cromwell and the daughters of her neighbours, the Throckmorton family, in Warboys.

The trouble had started when Jane, the youngest of the Throckmorton girls, began to suffer from seizures, in which her body would become convulsed and she would cry out hysterically. She claimed she could feel insects crawling all over her body and that a cat was clawing at her face. Unable to find a cause, the local doctor declared that she must be bewitched. Unfortunately, their neighbour Alice Samuel chose an inopportune moment to pay a call soon afterwards. As she sat down, Jane cried out: 'Did you ever seen anyone more like a witch than she is? I cannot abide to look on her.'

Things soon escalated. Perhaps jealous of all the attention Jane was getting, her two older sisters, Elizabeth and Mary, also began to

The witches' sabbat. Images like these helped fuel the fear of witchcraft in past centuries. *iStock*

exhibit hysterical behaviour and they too openly accused Mrs Samuel of being the witch responsible. Jane added that it was Mrs Samuel's intention to curse every woman in the house. The hysteria caught on and the female servants pleaded for Mrs Samuel to be dealt with, 'for she will kill us all if you let her alone'.

Lady Cromwell visited the house in Warboys and was shocked by the state of the Throckmorton girls. She insisted on speaking to Mrs Samuel (who was her tenant) and accused her to her face of being a witch. This Mrs Samuel hotly denied, becoming distressed at Lady Cromwell's obvious fear of her. 'Why are you afraid of me for I have never harmed you yet?' she said. The 'yet' was unfortunate. Even more unfortunate was the fact that Lady Cromwell also started suffering nightmares featuring attacks by cats and, after an illness, she died the following year.

Trouble at the Throckmortons' continued and Mrs Samuel found herself a virtual prisoner there. The girls remained calm and sober when she was in the house but as soon as she tried to leave, they became hysterical again. All this seemed proof of Mrs Samuel's guilt and in time the strain got to her too. She came to believe that she must be a witch without really knowing it. She effectively confessed to being so. However, after questioning by the authorities, she was allowed home, where her husband and daughter talked sense into her and begged her to retract her statement. She did so, but with the tragic result that the authorities now implicated her family in the alleged plot. Eventually, they all came to trial and were found guilty.

In 1659 an extraordinary document appeared boldly entitled *Strange and Terrible Newes from Cambridge*. It was one of many published at about the same time that took the form of bizarre and bigoted diatribes against the Society of Friends: the Quakers. Quakers were regarded with the same suspicion as Roman Catholics by certain sections of the fanatically Protestant society of the time and they were often accused of all manner of crimes and cruelties, including human sacrifice and devil worship.

Strange and Terrible Newes tells a tall tale of one Mary Philips who fell in with the Quakers for a spell (literally), before returning to the comforting bosom of the Church of England. Mary made a wild accusation against the leaders of the local Society of Friends, Robert Dickson and Jane Cranaway. She said that, in revenge for her turning away from Quakerism, Dickson and Cranaway used magic to transform her into a horse. They then rode her to a meeting near Cambridge. On being returned to human form, Mary went to the authorities, citing as evidence for her ludicrous story bruises on her hands and feet, tears in her dress and cuts in her side which she said were made by the Quakers' spurs. Dickson and Cranaway were arrested by the credulous constables but were later released.

Strange & Terrible

NEVVES

FROM

CAMBRIDGE,

BEING

A true *Relation* of the *Quakers* bewitching of *Mary Philips* out of the Bed from her Huf-
band in the Night, and transformed her into the
fhape of a Bay Mare, riding her from
Dinton, towards the *Univerfity*.

With the manner how fhe became
vifible again to the People in her own Likneneſs and
Shape, with her fides all rent and torn, as if they
had been fpur-gal'd, her hands and feet worn
as black as a Coal, and her mouth flit with
the Bridle Bit.

Likewife, her *Speech* to the *Scholars*
and *Countrey-men*, upon this great and wonderful *Change*,
her Oath before the Judges and Juftices, **and he**
Names of the *Quakers* brought to Tryal on *Friday* laft at the Affifes held at *Cambridge*. With
the Judgment of the *Court*.
As alfo, the Devils fnatching of one from his Company, and
hoifting of him up into the *Air*, with what hapned
thereupon.

London, Printed for *C. Brooks,* and are to be fold at the
Royal Exchange in *Cornhill,* 1659.

This 17th-century publication told a bizarre account of a woman who
claimed to have been turned into a horse and ridden to Black Masses

SOME LOCAL WITCHES

In addition to the grim history of the witch trials, there is a wealth of folklore devoted to supposed witches active in Cambridgeshire until quite recent times. In 1915, a Miss Catherine Parsons entertained the Cambridgeshire Antiquarian Society with tales about witches from her home village of Horseheath. She interviewed the oldest villager and learnt from them that Horseheath was formerly the home of an unnerving woman known by the strange name of 'Daddy Witch'. Miss Parsons was told that Daddy Witch had been 'an ancient bony creature, half-clad in rags', who had lived in a hut by a sheep-pond. She was known to have gained much of her knowledge of magic from a book called *The Devil's Plantation*.

When Daddy Witch died, her body was refused burial in consecrated ground and instead a grave was made for it in the middle of the road leading to Horseheath Green. It was said that the outline of her grave was frequently visible because her body was still warm and the road always remained dry over it. Twenty years later, it was still the custom for people using the road to nod their head nine times before passing over Daddy Witch's grave, in order to bring good luck or, perhaps more likely, to appease the witch's spirit and ward off bad luck.

Miss Parsons also unearthed several accounts at Horseheath regarding witches' familiars, or 'imps' as they were more generally called in Cambridgeshire. It was popularly believed that witches had as companions demons in animal form that would do their bidding, carrying out all manner of sinister tasks. They were even believed to 'suckle' these familiars from various parts of their bodies. At the height of the witch mania, any lonely or ill-favoured old woman might find herself targeted as a witch, and many would have owned a pet or two. More often than not these harmless animals would immediately be thought of as familiars and their keeping even used as evidence against their owners.

Miss Parsons relates a story about a witch in Horseheath asking the rag-and-bone man about the route he was about to take, but he refused to tell her, suspicious as to her motives. Sometime later, the rag-and-bone man heard something rustling in the hedge behind him, apparently following his cart. He swung round in time to see one of the witch's imps creeping through the undergrowth, presumably sent to keep tabs on him. He jumped down from his cart and tried to catch it, but the creature eluded him. He chased after it, but it scampered away, keeping just ahead of his grasp all

An old illustration of a witch tending to her familiars, which in this case took the form of toads

the way back to the witch's cottage. The witch was standing in her doorway waiting for her familiar. It sprang into her hands and she hid it in her bosom.

Once a witch had accepted the responsibility of owning familiars, it was almost impossible to get rid of them again. She would have to pass them on to a willing relative before she would be allowed to die. A witch of Horseheath received her imps from her sister after she died. They were called Bonny, Blue Cap, Red Cap, Jupiter and Venus and arrived in a tightly bound box, the interior of which no one was allowed to see except the witch. A few villagers did get a glimpse of the familiars, though, and to them they appeared to be quite ordinary white mice.

An elderly West Wickham woman, recorded as still being alive in the early 20th century, had no one to whom she could pass on her imps. She became tired of life, however, and determined to get rid of them. She heated up her oven and then shoved the imps inside it, hoping that they would be roasted to death. They squealed so furiously, however, that she felt compelled to take them back out again. Her familiars were entirely unharmed but in attempting to remove them, their owner burned herself badly and soon afterwards died. Her relatives buried the imps, still alive and thriving, in the grave along with their mistress.

In addition to female witches, there were also male wizards. Jabez Few, of Willingham, claimed to be a wizard and he too was possessed of imps. On one occasion he brought them into one of the village pubs. The drinkers in the bar heard them running up and down the stairs, but when they opened the door at the foot of the staircase, there was nothing to be seen.

Jabez used his imps to spy on people. He put one of them in the bedchamber of a Willingham woman named Connie Todd. She complained to her landlord, 'Old Man Dudley', and he was advised to 'get a big tom-cat' to catch the imp (perhaps it too was a mouse). Mr Dudley acquired a ginger tomcat and he shut it in the room. Behind the door he soon heard savage yowling and the sounds of fierce fighting. He looked in to see fur all over the floor and the cat 'flying up and down the curtains'. But he failed to catch the imp.

Someone with a knowledge of witchcraft told Mr Dudley that the only way to bring Jabez and his familiar into line was to create a 'witch bottle'. These bottles contained a foul mixture of substances – the ingredients varied – and were often buried under the hearthstone or outside the entrances of homes to ward off witches.

Many of the imps owned by Cambridgeshire witches looked suspiciously like white mice. *iStock*

Mr Dudley was advised to put the legs of a toad and the clippings from a horse's hoof in his bottle (he actually used a stone jar) and to put it on the fire. If the jar didn't break, Jabez's spell would and the imp would be removed or killed. Somehow Jabez learnt what Mr Dudley was doing and he turned up at the house before the jar was ready for the fire. He whistled loudly and the imp slunk out 'as meek as anything'.

To give an indication of how long such beliefs lingered, it is worth noting that Jabez Few died as recently as the 1920s. His imps were passed to his nephew, who didn't want them. To get rid of them, he gathered them up and then stood in the middle of a stream. Running water is inimical to evil spirits and the imps soon fled away, never to trouble anyone again.

A witch bottle explodes after being placed on the fire

POWER OVER BEASTS

A common belief in Cambridgeshire is that some people have an uncanny ability to control animals. Witches, of course, used this power maliciously. Old Bet Cross, a supposed witch living in Longstanton in the 19th century, could make any horse stop dead in its tracks. Watching the frustrated carters with glee, Old Bet would eventually show herself and cackle: 'It's no use you beatin' them 'orses because they can't go till I lets them!'

A Miss Disbury, of Willingham, who died around 1901, was said to have the same power. Enid Porter was told that on one occasion a herd of cows being driven past Miss Disbury's cottage suddenly came to a halt and refused to move any further along the lane, no matter how much they were beaten or cajoled. The drovers immediately put the blame on Miss Disbury. It was a long-held belief that the only way to rob a witch of her power – at least temporarily – was to draw her blood. One of the young men determined to break the spell, as he explained to Mrs Porter:

'So I goes up to her house, knocks on the door an' says: "Can you let me have a match, Miss Disbury?" Well, when she goes inside to fetch it, I gets out my shut-knife, open it when she comes back and hands me the match, I give her a slash across the wrist then I runs like hell. But those cows moved all right after that.'

At one time horses were absolutely essential to the rural economy. Before the advent of the petrol engine they were the main form of motive power and continued to be important for decades afterwards. Cambridgeshire was once possessed of an intriguing cabal of men who, like the American 'horse whisperers', had a peculiar affinity with horses. They could control them as they wished, including making them stay still in their tracks in the same way that witches were said to do. Indeed there was more than a hint of witchery about these men.

They were known as 'Toadmen' because the source of their power was the bone of a toad, which they would keep on them at all times. This bone came to them through an elaborate and rather gruesome magical ritual. In order to become a Toadman they would first have to catch a toad and then either skin it alive or peg it out on an ant heap until the ants had devoured it. Then the Toadman would gather up its skeleton and place it in his pocket, until the bones had dried out and become disjointed. At midnight on a night of the full moon he would carry the bones to a running stream and throw them into the water. They were said to emit a bloodcurdling scream as they hit the water. One of the bones would detach itself and begin to float away upstream against the flow of water. This was the magical bone and the Toadman had to be sharp-eyed and act quickly to snatch it out of the stream.

According to one account, the man now had to visit the stables three midnights in a row, with the bone in his pocket. On the third visit the Devil would appear and would draw his blood. The initiation was now complete, and he had been made a Toadman.

A farmer near Wisbech in the 1870s had the reputation of being a Toadman. It was a common procedure for him to pay a carter to take a load of corn to the market at Wisbech, but on one occasion he caught the man piling up straw on top of it which he intended to sell for himself. This was not the done thing, and when the carter tried to take the wagon to Wisbech, the horses refused to move. The farmer stuck his head out of the window and told him: 'Take off that bunch of straw, then they'll go.'

The carter begrudgingly removed his straw and sure enough the animals began to placidly pull the wagon. The carter stopped them round a bend in the road, where they were out of sight of the farmer. Then he sneaked back and gathered up his straw. He loaded the wagon with it – but the horses once again refused to budge. Eventually, the deceitful carter had no choice but to throw his straw into the dyke. Once he had done so, the horses continued to trot on to market.

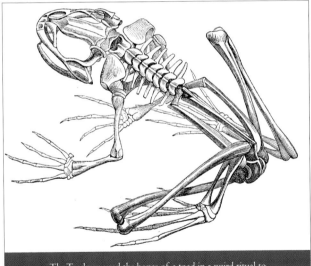

The Toadmen used the bones of a toad in a weird ritual to gain their strange power. *iStock*

EERIE STORIES

Gathered round the firelight after dark in houses and inns before the days of electricity or even gas lighting, it was natural for people to tell tales of the supernatural.

The churchyard is the setting for a similarly jovial yarn collected by members of Balsham's Women's Institute in 1956. One evening in the 19th century, some boozers in the White Lion started boasting about their bravery. One of them said he was willing to bet no one would have the guts to enter the churchyard, jump into the grave that had just been dug for one of their recently departed compatriots and bring back a skull. He added that it should be no trouble finding one, because the sexton was 'always digging up old bones when digging'.

One of the drinkers, full of Dutch courage, took up the challenge, however, and said he would go the very next night and bring back a headbone as proof. The following night, he was as good as his word, and made his way to the churchyard, unaware that one of the other men who been present in the pub had made up his mind to find out just how brave he really was. He got there ahead of him, and hid behind a tombstone. He watched as his friend clambered into the open grave and after a while emerged with a skull in his hand.

'Drop that, that's mine,' said the man behind the tombstone.

'Damn you,' said his friend in the grave. 'I know that's a lie, for you never had two heads!'

Another tongue-in-cheek yarn involves the discovery of Roman remains, including two skeletons, at Whittlesford in the 1820s. In his *Cambridgeshire Cameos* of 1895, author W.R. Brown wrote: 'There is an amusing story told in the village about one of these skeletons. It was one of two which were discovered in a most remarkable position, showing that they were combatants; one was gripping the other so tightly that even in the grave they were not separated.

'This particular skeleton was in a sitting posture; one of the venturesome labourers took a fancy to the skull of this warrior, and accordingly dismembered it from the skeleton and carried it home to his cottage. At night, however, up came the headless skeleton to the labourer's house. Knocking at the door, it demanded restitution of the skull. This occurred night after night, so the gossips say, until the skull was taken back and replaced.'

The Fenland of Cambridgeshire, which at one time was much more extensive, was the perfect environment in which to create marsh gas. The methane had a tendency to ignite, creating eerie floating lights glimpsed among the sedge. Such phenomena were believed to be evil spirits and bringers of misfortune.

The phenomena were known variously Will-o'-the-Wisps, Hob o'-Lantern or Lantern Men. In Cambridgeshire they were also known by the more disparaging term of Jenny Burnt Arses.

Another spooky feature of Cambridgeshire folklore is the huge spectral hound known as Black Shuck. Similar ghosts are claimed for almost every English county, with many other examples in Wales and Scotland, too. They all have similarities, such as being huge in size, more or less canine in appearance, often with shaggy coats,

A traveller follows a Will-o'-the-Wisp through the dark countryside

and with unearthly features such as being headless or possessing glowing red eyes. They also share the common characteristic of following benighted travellers along lonely roads and paths.

Some think the belief in them dates back to the Anglo-Saxon period because their god Woden was said to be accompanied by a monstrous black dog. The mysterious, still uncatchable black panthers supposed to roam wild places like Dartmoor and Bodmin Moor may merely be a modern interpretation of these enigmatic apparitions. 'Big as a calf [and] quiet as death' is how one old countryman described the appearance of Black Shuck as it padded along the causeway through Wicken Fen. The horrible hound was

Sherlock Holmes and Dr Watson catch sight of The Hound of the Baskervilles in Conan Doyle's famous story. This fictional hound was inspired by legends of spectral black dogs such as those encountered in Cambridgeshire also believed to patrol lanes or footpaths at West Wickham, West Wratting and Balsham and also the Devil's Ditch, an ancient earthwork at Reach. He was even seen in Cambridge, leaping over the bonnet of a car in Arbury Road. An early motor car apparently ran over Black Shuck in 1906. The driver collided with something huge and black in the fog on a minor road which runs alongside the River Ouse near Littleport. He stopped his vehicle and got down but could find nothing in the road or alongside it. He did not know that the spot where the collision took place had been a known haunt of Black Shuck, nor that the haunting ceased after the accident.

The Caxton Gibbet is one of Cambridgeshire's most grisly landmarks. It stands beside a roundabout on the A428 from Cambridge to St Neots. It's a modern replica but at one time criminals' bodies really were hung in chains here as a deterrent to other would-be felons. Once upon a time an inn stood facing the gibbet on the other side of what was then a crossroads.

There are a number of stories about this gibbet. Some say it was originally erected to expose the body of a notorious highwayman named Gatwood, who was hanged in 1753 for robbing mail coaches on the Great North Road; others that three men were hanged from it for sheep-stealing and that they were then buried beneath it.

Much more colourful is the yarn about a murderous landlord of the inn which used to stand opposite the Caxton Gibbet. He made a good living from customers who came to watch the hangings or simply to stare at the remains of the criminals swinging in the iron cage. However, this wasn't enough for him. He also had the habit of robbing and then doing away with lonely travellers who looked like they might have a full purse. One fateful night, he overreached himself. He crept into the room used by lodgers, intending to steal the purse from one of three men sleeping there. However, one of the other boarders woke up and saw what he was doing. Before the man could raise the alarm, the innkeeper stabbed him through the heart with his knife. He then dispatched the other two while they slept so that there would be no witnesses. The murderer tried to hide all three bodies in a well but it wasn't long before his crime was discovered.

A few weeks later it was the innkeeper's turn to hang in chains from the Caxton Gibbet. His execution drew quite a crowd and the new landlord did well out of his predecessor's execution. For years afterwards, the inn was said to be haunted by the killer's ghost. Many people claimed to hear disembodied footsteps and sounds like a body being dragged down the stairs and along a passageway to the well.

There is one more legend associated with the Caxton Gibbet. This involved the murder of a man named Partridge several hundred years ago. Mr Partridge's body was found in a place called Monk Field, at Bourn, but his killer was never caught. One day, many years after the event, a stranger came to the inn at Caxton, spending liberally and drinking with some abandon. The villagers found he was good for a free drink or two and gathered round him. It soon became apparent that although he was unfamiliar to them, he knew the area pretty well. After name-dropping various local characters and places, he then told the gathered crowd how he had once robbed a nest of partridges but had managed to avoid being caught by the gamekeepers. He seemed unnecessarily proud of this minor triumph and leered suggestively at the crowd as he related it.

The innkeeper had been listening to the stranger's boasting and in a flash he suddenly remembered the unsolved Partridge murder and

The Caxton Gibbet is the focus for a number of gruesome stories.
iStock

realised the true meaning behind this apparently harmless anecdote. He sent for the police. Not only the stranger's boasting but also a distinctive birthmark gave him away as the murderer. After being found guilty at his trial, he was strapped into an iron cage, suspended from the Caxton Gibbet and left to die a slow and agonising death from starvation.

An addition to the story is that a baker passing by the gibbet was so moved to pity by the criminal's pitiful cries for sustenance, that he gave him a loaf of bread. This act of kindness was strictly against the law, however, and the unfortunate baker was promptly hanged from the gibbet beside the murderer.

SUPERSTITIONS

Before the second half of the 20th century, our rural ancestors were far closer to the land and much more aware of the changing seasons, nuances in the weather and the flora and fauna around them than the vast majority of us are today. However, this intimate knowledge was contrasted with a series of superstitions earnestly believed in without having any basis in fact.

There were a number of strange beliefs, for example, about the moon. It was considered unlucky to see the new moon through glass. It was always better to see it for the first time in the open air. The waxing and waning of the moon was thought to affect not only the tides but the growth of all living things. In the days when blood-letting was commonly used by physicians to treat all sorts of ailments, it was believed that blood too had a tide affected by the moon. It was therefore thought best drained at the waxing of the moon to help draw out the badness believed to be in it. A child born under a waning moon would grow up to be less healthy, it was thought, than one born when the moon was waxing. Likewise, animals tended to be slaughtered when the moon was increasing, otherwise the meat might shrink when it was cooked.

The behaviour of birds and animals was taken to have special meaning, in superstitions perhaps dating back to our pagan past. An inexplicable belief about the hare was recorded in Cambridgeshire in the 1890s. *The Fenland Notes and Queries* of 1891 noted the following rhyme from Peterborough:

If in the minster close a hare
Should for itself have made a lair,
Be sure before the week is down
A fire will rage within the town.

Why the appearance of a hare like this should be a warning of fire is anybody's guess, and yet a similar superstition pertained to Ramsey, too:

Should a hare in hasty flight
Scamper through Ramsey Whyte
Be sure three days are gone
A fire will blaze in Ramsey town.

'Ramsey Whyte' refers to the ruined gatehouse of Ramsey Abbey.

More understandable was the huddling together of livestock observed at Bourn on 4 May 1800. It was an unseasonably hot day, and unnaturally calm. In the early afternoon the cattle in the fields were seen to 'assemble in groups', as an observer put it, while others took themselves off to their byres unbidden, found refuge in barns or gathered close to the hedges. They 'bellowed extremely' for an hour or two and then, just after 2pm, great black clouds rolled in, so dense that it was as if the day had turned to night. There soon followed a devastating deluge of rain and hail, accompanied by high winds and lightning. Somehow the cattle had sensed the oncoming storm and had taken their own precautions. It is said animals are able to sense earthquakes ahead of human beings – and even seismographs – in much the same way.

At one time anglers believed that the behaviour of cattle reflected the likelihood or otherwise of catching fish. If the cattle were grazing, angling would be successful because the fish too would be feeding, but if they were lying down, the fish would be skulking away at the bottom of the streams, chewing the cud, so to speak.

There are numerous weather superstitions in old country lore, which is hardly surprising since the weather affected rural communities so significantly. Some of these pertained to wildlife. It was said, for example, that to hear a cuckoo stammer foretold coming rain, as did the screeching of a peacock. Rooks massing together while feeding and dogs eating grass were also thought to be an indicator of wet weather. Swallows flying high indicated warm, fine weather, but if they flew low, it would be wet (no doubt this was truly indicated by the position in the atmosphere of the insects on which they were feeding). In regards to trees, it was also believed a wet spring was bound to follow if the leaves on the ash trees emerged before those of the oak. As a popular rhyme had it:

> If the ash is out before the oak,
> Look out, you'll get a soak.

In winter, if a cat was seen to turn her back on the fire and warm her behind, it was a warning that snow was on its way. A fire burning with a blue flame was also thought to indicate snow. A white hoar frost was supposed to warn of a coming storm. The whiter the frost, the more severe the storm. Some people called the sun's rays when they fell on rivers or ponds 'the sun's water pipes' and believed that the sun was replenishing its water pots with them. As soon as the pots were filled, it would pour them down as rain.

A hare making its lair in the close at Peterborough Cathedral was for some inexplicable reason seen as an omen that fire would break out in the city.
iStock

Almost everyone knows the old saw: 'Red sky at night, shepherd's delight; Red sky at morning, shepherd's warning.' Another rhyme gives the same virtue of predicting rain or shine to rainbows:

Rainbow in the morning,
Shepherds take warning;
Rainbow afternoon,
Good weather coming soon;
Rainbow at night,
Shepherd's delight.

It is difficult to know how a rainbow can be seen at night unless it's round the moon. Possibly the rhyme is referring to late summer's evenings. A more comprehensive, if even less likely, litany of rainbow superstitions can be found in the following rhyme:

Rainbow in the south, heavy rain and snow;
Rainbow in the west, little showers and dew;
Rainbow in the east, fair skies and blue;
Rainbow to windward, foul falls the day;
Rainbow to leeward, damp runs away.

It was considered unlucky to point at a rainbow. One superstition stated that the arm used to point with would become paralysed as a result. There was a whole host of superstitions in which animals and birds were supposed to be lucky or unlucky. You will already be familiar with the rhyme about magpies: 'One for sorrow, two for joy etc.' It was said that if a crow crossed your path from left to right, this was a warning of coming misfortune, but if it crossed in the opposite direction, this was a good omen. A raven flying over a house or a robin flying into a house were both considered unlucky. The screech of a barn owl and a dog howling at night were both bad omens, as was a cock crowing at night, or laying an egg, or a hen laying unusually small eggs. Bees swarming on a Sunday also brought bad luck.

Even pretty flowers could be looked on askance. It was a fairly universal belief that hawthorn (may) blossom would bring bad luck if it was brought into the house, and some said the same of snowdrops. Even the daffodil, that cheerful bloom which brightens many a home in early spring, had a bad reputation. It was forbidden in any household where chickens, ducks or geese were kept because it was believed the flowers would prevent them laying. Catkins would not only stop hens laying but any livestock giving birth until they were removed.

That so many superstitions pertained to bad luck rather than to good suggests our ancestors generally had a pessimistic outlook. It's a hint perhaps at just how uncertain and brief people's lives were in the past, before modern medicine existed or was freely available.

Our rural ancestors employed a whole range of folk remedies to try to cure themselves of any ailments that might afflict them. No doubt some of these, employing medicinal herbs, were genuinely efficacious, and an old belief that a spider's web wrapped round a cut would help heal it turned out to be true after penicillin was discovered: webs are often full of it. Many other remedies seemed logical but have no basis in modern medicine. Medieval herbalists believed in 'the doctrine of signatures', choosing herbs that vaguely resembled the parts of the body they hoped they'd treat. For example, lungwort, whose leaves resemble lungs, was presumed to be good for respiratory problems. Unfortunately, this optimistic approach rarely proved helpful.

Another commonly held belief was that a person's illness could be transferred to a living animal. For example, a ritual involved placing

May blossom is one of the cheering sights of early summer but woe betide anyone who brought any into their home. *iStock*

a live spider inside a walnut shell and then hanging this round the sick person's neck. As the spider died, so would the illness. A popular method to remove warts involved rubbing the warts with a snail and then sticking the unfortunate creature on a hawthorn. As the snail rotted away, so would the warts. People seemed to be particularly bothered by warts in the past and there are numerous 'cures' on record to get rid of them. Another ritual involved laying a bag on a path containing the same number of grains of wheat or of pennies as the person had warts. Anyone foolish enough to pick up the bag would have the warts transferred to them.

Some folk remedies were even more bizarre. Moss found growing on a skull in a graveyard, if dried, ground and taken as snuff, was supposed to cure headaches. A fried mouse in breadcrumbs was given as a meal to children to cure them of wetting the bed. In the hope of taking away the dangerous disease of whooping cough, some people would clip off a lock of the hair of the afflicted child, make a sandwich of it and then feed it to a dog. There was no suggestion that the disease would be transferred to the animal, as in the examples above, but nevertheless this odd custom was believed to at least ease the cough. An even weirder remedy for whooping cough involved the catching of a trout (it had to be caught not bought), cooking it in cider and then cutting off the head. The head was placed inside the sick child's mouth, the fish's jaws outermost, and the child was then instructed to breathe through it!

In addition to these largely unaccountable remedies were charms, in the form of little prayers, that would be uttered by the sufferer or by those trying to help him. A charm for stopping the flow of blood, either after a wound or injury, or perhaps simply in the case of a nosebleed, went:

'In the name of the Father and of the Son and of the Holy Ghost – Christ was born at Bethlehem – dipped in the river Jordan – blessed that river and so it stood. So our Lord Jesus stop this blood.'

This approach was particularly popular for toothache. A typical charm was:

'Peter sat at the gates of Jerusalem. Jesus Christ came by and said, "What ailest thou?" "My teeth and bones do ache full sore." He said, "Thy teeth and bones shall ache no more."'

In some versions Peter was replaced with the name of the sufferer. The charm might also be written out on a piece of paper, folded up and then worn round the neck until the toothache abated. Clearly, these charms had little to do with orthodox Christian theology but must have brought some comfort to the faithful.

Moss scraped from a skull found in a graveyard was one of the more grisly ingredients used in folk medicine. *iStock*

GOOD LUCK

According to our rural ancestors, if you want to ensure good luck then DO:

Carry a piece of coal in your pocket

Carry a piece of iron with a hole in it

Carry a rabbit's foot

Keep a lock of hair from a baby's first haircut

Burn your tea leaves

Salute a solitary magpie

Wish on a falling star

Bow nine times to the new moon

Cut your fingernails on a Thursday

Put on your left sock or stocking first when getting dressed

Pick up a pin if you see one

Pick up a white stone, spit on it and throw it over your head

Take a snail by its horns and throw it backwards over your shoulder

Throw a pinch of salt over your left shoulder

Begin a journey with your right foot first

Look for a four-leaved clover

Look for a double-leaved sprig of ash

Let a black cat cross your path

Nail up a horseshoe, with the points upwards

Cross your fingers if you accidentally do anything unlucky

BAD LUCK

According to our rural ancestors, if you want to avoid bad luck then DON'T:

Walk under a ladder

Put shoes or boots on the table

Shake hands across the table

Spill salt on the table

Sing at the table

Sleep on the table

Place your knife and fork crossways on your plate

Turn your bed on a Sunday

Brush the dust out of the front door

Give gloves as a present

Cut your fingernails on a Monday, Friday or Sunday

Open an umbrella in the house

Bring thyme into the house

Carry anything on your shoulder in the house

Enter a house for the first time through the back door

Throw dead flowers onto the fire

Cut down a flowering tree

Turn back after beginning a journey

Do anything on Friday 13th

Nail up a horseshoe with the points down, so all the luck drains out

THE JOURNEY
THROUGH LIFE

Life was more precarious in the past. The lack of understanding as to what caused diseases or the knowledge of how to cure them meant mortality rates were high, especially among children. For the same reason, accidents involving injury were also far more serious. Wars were more frequent, too.

The perilous journey through life had important stages which were celebrated with ritual and accompanied by superstition. There were several strange beliefs regarding the beginning of life. It was said that a child born at midnight would have second sight and that a 'footling', that is one born feet first, would have magical powers. Efforts were made to preserve the caul surrounding the child at birth because it was thought to be possessed with sympathetic magic. Kept safe, it would prevent the person it belonged to ever suffering death by drowning. There are records well into the 20th century of sailors buying cauls in the belief they would keep them safe.

As soon as the mother entered labour, a party would be held at her house called a Merry Meet. The prospective husband would entertain family and neighbours and a 'groaning cheese' and a 'groaning cake' would be carefully cut into exactly the right number of pieces to serve to the guests. Unfortunately, of course, the woman giving birth was unable to enjoy the festivities herself.

At one time new mothers genuinely feared their children might be stolen by fairies unless they protected them with certain charms before they were baptised.

With infant mortalities being so high, it was considered essential to christen the new-born baby as soon as possible. An unbaptised child would not go to heaven, but some thought they might become fairies instead. If the baptism was performed at home, the water used to christen the child was often thrown into the fire, to ensure it remained pure and that no evil influence could pollute it. While it was still unbaptised, it was customary to present the baby with an egg, symbolising new life, some salt and, unsafe though it may seem, a box of matches. Salt and fire were considered sure charms against the attentions of evil spirits.

Even after baptism, the infant might be at threat from fairies, who were thought to cast envious eyes at human children. To ward them off parents might hang over the crib a pair of scissors or tongs, which would dangle in the form of a cross. The cross-shape and the iron in the scissors were sure protection against the 'little people'. If fairies did get their hands on a baby, they would leave in its place a 'changeling', a peevish and ugly fairy child, or a block of wood so enchanted as to resemble the stolen infant. Babies who succumbed to what today we call cot-death were often thought to be the lifeless substitute left behind by kidnapping fairies.

An amusing superstition of the past saw some mothers biting their children's fingernails short rather than cutting them. They believed that if they cut the fingernails, the child would grow up to be a thief. It was also said that a new baby must always be carried upstairs before it goes down, otherwise it would not rise in life. If there were no stairs in the house, the midwife would climb onto a chair with it.

Moving on to young adulthood, there were also some interesting customs surrounding courtship. We tend to assume morals were more conservative in the past, so it may be a surprise to learn that courting couples were often allowed to sleep together undisturbed. However, this was only with the proviso that the young man kept his clothes on (minus his coat and boots). A variant custom called 'bundling' allowed the couple to share a bed with a bolster between them. Such would have been the disgrace if the young couple abused this trust that few did. Mind you, engagements tended to be shorter then.

A young woman hoping to marry into a farming family was often called upon to prove her strength by lifting with one arm the heavy lid of the parish chest in the church. The parish chest contained charitable donations and other valuables and was usually made of thick oak, bound with stout iron. To lift it with just one arm could be quite a feat.

As to the wedding day itself, there was an ancient custom in which the friends of the groom would call at the bride's house with the view of 'abducting' her. Her duty was to hide, so as to avoid this indignity, or better still to sneak to church before they caught her. This was a remnant of a custom known thousands of years ago in which young men would prove their worth by stealing the girl they fancied from under her parents' roof. In more civilised times, no abduction or manhandling of the bride actually took place and the whole thing was done in fun.

A rather unkind superstition related to weddings was that if a woman served as a bridesmaid three times, she would never be married herself. Likewise, a man who acted as best man three times would never wed. But there are even stranger ones on record:

If a young woman puts on a man's hat or a young man puts on a woman's hat, they will have to wait three years before they can get married.

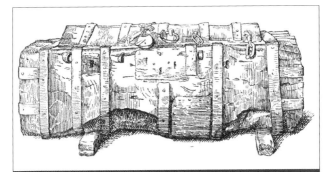

An example of a parish chest, an ancient and massive casket sometimes carved out of one solid piece of oak. Lifting its heavy lid with one arm would be hard work for most men, let alone the young women who were expected to do it

If a young person cuts bread obliquely or in uneven slices they will never be married, or will have to wait seven years, or they will end up with an objectionable mother-in-law.

If while sweeping a girl touches the foot of another girl with a broom she will rob that girl of her future husband.

When the bride enters the church, she must never look behind her or she will end up regretting the marriage.

There are equally strange superstitions regarding the really great change in a person's life – death. In the 'Superstitions' chapter several unlucky signs and portents were referred to, such as dogs howling and owls screeching, and these might equally be taken as omens of a coming death. There are many more. Clocks suddenly stopping or chiming thirteen were a bad sign, as were a robin tapping at the window pane, a crow getting into the house or an owl settling on the roof. Mysterious noises such as knocks and raps in the house where someone lay ill were also ominous. Carpenters sometimes claimed they had heard sounds in their workshops at night resembling those of a coffin being made. They knew then that one would soon be ordered.

When the last moment had apparently come, people were sometimes 'helped to die' by those looking after them. All the doors and windows in the house were opened wide to allow the soul to escape. At the same time, knots were untied, mirrors covered and the fire – the 'soul of the house' – was put out. 'Passing bells' were traditionally rung nine times to announce a death but their original purpose was to scare away any evil spirits seeking to claim the soul of the departed. A plate of salt, that substance long believed to ward off evil, was placed on the body. No corpse was left with its eyes open for it was said that it would be looking for the next person to die.

After a death, the household would 'keep watch' for at least one night while the corpse lay in the house because it was thought that the soul of the departed might return. Sometimes the assembly would chant: 'It is for the last time, it is the last night', in order to remind the spirit that it had to pass on.

If the master of the house died, it was considered important to inform the bees in the hive of the fact, otherwise they'd all fly away. Any significant tree or bush, even household plants, were at one time draped with black crepe after a death, otherwise it was feared they would wither away.

Once the corpse was conveyed to the burial place, it had to be taken to its grave in the same direction as the sun passes through the sky, that is 'deseal' or 'deosil'. To take it in the opposite direction, 'widdershins', would make the soul vulnerable to malign forces.

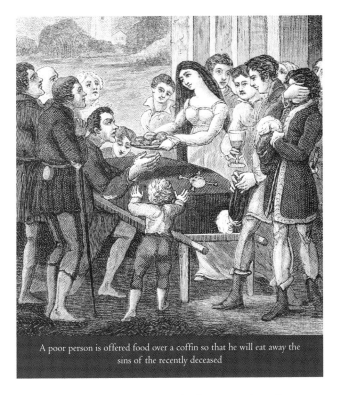

A poor person is offered food over a coffin so that he will eat away the sins of the recently deceased

There was a prejudice about being the first person buried in a new graveyard, because it was said that the Devil had the right to claim the first corpse. Another superstition had it that the spirit of the most recent person to be buried haunted the graveyard, watching over it until another burial took place.

A decidedly primitive custom, which had all but died out by the end of the 19th century, was that of the 'sin-eater'. The sin-eater was usually a poor member of the parish who was prepared, for a small fee and a meal, to spiritually take on the sins of the person who had just died. This would be achieved by offering the man specially baked cakes, or bread on a dish of salt, the eating of which meant that he would absorb the sins. The food might even be offered over the coffin of the dead; at any rate it would always be eaten in the graveyard. This belief seems to hark back to the time when our most distant ancestors believed they could take on the power and attributes of a deceased person by devouring their body. The sin-eater was therefore a kind of spiritual cannibal.

THROUGH THE SEASONS

The rural calendar was marked by a series of high days and festivals intended to mark crucial times for sowing, reaping and other agricultural activities. These were often of great antiquity, pre-dating the Christian era. Many of them were adopted by the Church, although rededicated and renamed, and have therefore been preserved down the years.

The Celtic New Year was 1 November, when winter began. The coming dark days were defied with a great celebratory feast called Samhain. Bonfires were lit, animals were mated for the following spring and any surplus beasts slaughtered to fatten every one up in advance of the approaching cold. Guy Fawkes Night is a survival of the Samhain bonfire festival, merely put back a few days and given a political context which would have meant nothing to our pagan ancestors.

As a transient period, between the old year and the new, Samhain was considered a time when spirits from the underworld could revisit the earth. It was a time of ghosts and witches. This ancient belief is recalled in our still prevalent Halloween traditions. The Church diffused the apparent menace in this festival by dedicating 1 November to all the saints in heaven. 'Hallows' is an archaic word for 'saints', and Halloween is a contraction of 'All Hallows Eve', that is to say the night before All Hallows or All Saints Day. It was formerly the custom on 1 November to go Souling, roaming the parish in request of small gifts of money to be presented with specially baked dainties called soul cakes.

The next great festival in the Celtic calendar was Imbolc, on 1 February. This marked the beginning of the lambing season and is echoed in the Christian Feast of the Purification of the Virgin Mary, or Candlemas, celebrated the following day. Candlemas was dedicated to new mothers and childbirth.

The start of summer was celebrated on 1st May, in the Celtic festival called Beltane. Given over to fertility and the reawakening of the earth, this was a free-for-all party, with singing, dancing, the lighting of more bonfires and a certain amount of licence. May Day continued the tradition in a diluted form. Dancing round the maypole, a pretty ritual, probably replaced a more ribald ceremony.

The last of the big four Celtic festivals took place on 1 August and was called Lugnasad. This was the harvest festival, when the grain would be gathered in. The Christianised Saxons knew it as *hlaf-maesse*, meaning 'loaf-mass', which has since become corrupted to Lammas or Lammastide. The first loaves of bread made from the

The charming custom of dancing round the maypole had its origin in a pagan fertility festival. *iStock*

gathered grain were dedicated to God in a more general Festival of the First Fruits.

In between these four seasonal festivals were many others, some of pagan and some of Christian origin, and others, like Easter and Christmas, a blend of the two. Lupercalia, the Roman celebration of youth, took place in the middle of February. In the warmer climes of the east it served as something of a harbinger of spring in which young people were encouraged to choose lovers. It had a reputation for excess, thoroughly defused by the adoption in its place of the feast honouring the martyrdom of St Valentine, which took place on 14 February. Valentine was a gentleman committed to chastity and it seems his association with romantic love was merely a matter of convenience. Nonetheless, St Valentine's Day remains one of the most popular traditions in the modern calendar, and people have been exchanging love tokens on this day for centuries.

Although Easter honours the Crucifixion and Resurrection of Christ, there are many secular traditions attached to it which date from pre-Christian times. Eggs are a natural symbol of rebirth and were equally appropriate for both the Resurrection and for spring, the season in which Easter falls. It was once a common pastime on Easter Day for people to roll gaily coloured hard-boiled eggs down hillsides in a jovial race. This was called 'pace-egging'. It has been suggested that the rolling eggs represented the life-giving sun's passage through the sky. It's likely that the name Easter has been borrowed from a pagan goddess of the spring, Eostre. The Easter Bunny may well be a descendant of the hare, an animal associated with the spring and fertility and sacred to the Celts.

'Lifting' was a widespread and peculiar custom carried out at Easter but which has now died out. It took place on Easter Monday and

Tuesday. A chair would be garlanded with flowers and people would take it in turns to sit in it while their fellows raised them into the air. It was common for men to lift women on Monday and the other way round on Tuesday. A charming performance in the villages, it could be a rowdy affair in towns, where strangers were sometimes bundled into the chair and forced to pay a fee in order to be let down again. Folklorist Christina Hole has this to say about lifting:

'The usual explanation was that it was done in memory of our Lord's rising, but it is more probable that it was a survival of an old agricultural rite. In Central Europe girls leap through decorated hoops, saying "Grow flax, grow" as they do it, and the higher they leap the taller the flax will be. Lifting may have originated in something of the same kind.'

Other traditions relating to Easter are inarguably Christian, however. On Good Friday, the day of Christ's Crucifixion, we still eat Hot Cross Buns. At one time it was common for all loaves to be marked

Hard-boiled 'pace eggs', brightly coloured with vegetable dyes, were rolled down hills in an old Easter custom. *iStock*

with a cross. Despite its name, Good Friday's association made it an unlucky one in the minds of our ancestors. It has become a bank holiday because those engaged in dangerous occupations, such as mining and fishing, refused to work on that day. Blacksmiths and those in the building trades would often down tools too because it was considered poor taste to handle nails on that day.

The following two days were quite different in character. Easter Sunday was always given over to worship and Monday was a holiday given over to leisure and sports. Some believed that the sun danced on Easter Day in joyous memory of the Resurrection and it was formerly a custom to rise before dawn in the hope of seeing this phenomenon. It was also traditional to wear new clothes on Easter Day, or at least one item that had never been worn before.

Beating the Bounds was another ritual commonly carried out at this time of the year, usually on Ascension Day (5 May). In the days before maps were freely available, it was important to clearly define parish boundaries and to ensure that nothing had occurred to alter them. Beating the Bounds was sometimes taken rather too literally, however. The villagers, accompanied by a clergyman, would take the young boys of the parish on a tour of the landmarks on its boundary. At each one they would pause and the boys would be whipped to make sure they remembered them. The clergyman would often bless the landmarks, too, especially wells.

The day before the feast of St John the Baptist, 23 June, or St John's Eve was known as Midsummer Eve, even though the Summer Solstice – the longest day of the year – falls a couple of days before. Once again, this important stage in the year was celebrated with the lighting of bonfires.

There were numerous customs and celebrations associated with the bringing in of the harvest in the autumn. Fairs and sales were held at Michaelmas, on 29 September.

The strange custom of Lifting was popular on Easter Monday and the following Tuesday but has now completely died out

The final great festival of the winter was, of course, Christmas. There is in fact no Biblical reference to the date of Christ's birthday and 25 December was chosen because it coincided with ancient pagan rituals associated with the Winter Solstice, the shortest day of the year, and with the birth dates of rival gods, such as Mithras: 25 December became the Festival of the Unconquered Sun during the reign of the Roman Emperor Aurelius. It made sense for the early Christians to adopt a day already given over to celebration, especially one relating to the sense of hope engendered by the start of longer days and shorter nights.

Many of the old, traditional customs associated with Christmas are of pre-Christian origin. Prince Albert, Queen Victoria's husband, is famously credited with bringing the custom of decorating a fir tree to Britain from his native Germany. In fact, there are records of an evergreen tree lit with candles being set up in a London street as long ago as the 15th century. This seems to have been a Norse tradition, as was the selecting of a Yule log, although the word 'Yule' has an Anglo-Saxon origin.

As we have seen, the lighting of fires was a central element to the ancient Celtic celebrations. Fire gave warmth and light, allowed food to be cooked and represented that great life-bringer, the sun. Fire therefore brought luck and scared away the powers of darkness. The Yule log would be selected with great ceremony and celebration, in much the way we would choose a Christmas tree today. The larger the fireplace, the larger the log chosen to fill it. Lighting the log became traditional on Christmas Eve and, if it was big enough, it might bring warmth throughout Christmas Day and beyond.

Holly became associated with Christmas because it is an evergreen, and mistletoe simply because it was the plant most sacred to our

Cutting and bringing home the Yule log was a major occasion in big houses during the run-up to Christmas. *iStock*

Celtic ancestors. According to a Roman historian, the Druids would only allow the plant to be cut with a golden sickle as it was so precious.

The Twelve Days of Christmas, which included our present New Year's Day and Twelfth Night (6 January), were the perfect excuse for having a good time. Where possible, big family gatherings would be held or feasts where the servants as well as the masters would be entertained. Carols would be sung by the poor, and extra pennies collected to help them celebrate later on. A more boisterous variant of carol singing was the traditional wassailing. 'Wassail' is an Old English word meaning 'be of good cheer'. Poor people would walk round the parish singing wassailing songs either for money or, more usually, for beer. Those better off might have in their possession a wassail cup, large and often of elaborate design, which they would fill with mulled beer or wine and use it to toast each other. Mummers Plays – medieval morality plays – were also performed in many places.

In a custom dating back to Roman times, the roles of master and servant were overturned on one day of the year around Christmas time, with the staff served a feast by their employers. Sometimes a Lord of Misrule might be appointed from among the servants, a kind of fool king. In some military regiments today the officers serve Christmas dinner to their men. A charming custom was to lay the table for two on Christmas Eve to 'welcome Joseph and Mary on Christmas morning'. There was also a superstition that animals were able to talk on Christmas morning and some people, particularly children, would creep to the pens and cowsheds as the sun rose in the hope of catching them doing so.

Finally, it was also traditional to celebrate New Year's Day with a party, reflecting the universal belief that it is lucky to begin anything in good spirits. Of course, this tradition still holds true today.

Mistletoe, an unusual plant that is a parasite on other trees, is now closely associated with Christmas but at one time it was venerated by the Druids.
iStock

More Legends & Folklore books from Bradwell Books for you to enjoy.

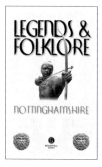

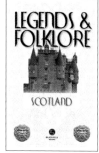

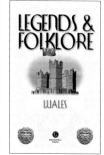

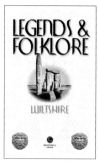

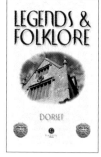

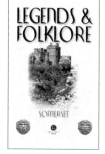

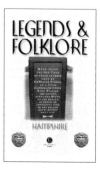

Visit www.bradwellbooks.co.uk for more details